MW01068871

8/3/17

Feed Your Vow

Dear Elizabeth,

I'm so very blessed
to have your touch on
my & my family's life.
I hope some of these
poems nourish & befriend
you well!

with love,

Brooke

Feed Your Vow
poems for falling into fullness

Brooke McNamara

Foreword by Stuart Davis

PERFORMANCE
INTEGRAL
Boulder, Colorado

All Rights Reserved
Copyright © 2015 Brooke McNamara

Performance Integral Edition
Copyright © 2015

No part of this book may be reproduced or transmitted in any form
or by any means, electronic or mechanical, including photocopying,
recording, or by any other information storage and retrieval system,
without permission in writing from the copyright owner.

Published by Performance Integral, Boulder, Colorado.
www.PerformanceIntegral.com
www.FeedYourVow.com

FIRST EDITION

Printed responsibly with the following sustainability certifications:
Sustainable Forest Initiative® SFI®
Endorsement of Forest Certification™ PEFC™
Forest Stewardship Council® FSC®

2 4 6 8 10 9 7 5 3 1

Cover Design by Alex Musat. www.alexmusat.com/portfolio
Cover Photo by Portia Snow.
Back Cover Headshot by Heather Gray.

LIBRARY OF CONGRESS CATALOGING-IN-PUBLICATION DATA

McNamara, Brooke J.   1981 -
     Feed Your Vow, Poems for Falling into Fullness / Brooke McNamara

ISBN-10: 0988768933
ISBN-13: 978-0-9887689-3-2

1. Poetry—General. 2. Poetry—Women Authors. 3. Body, Mind & Spirit—
Mindfulness.
4. I. Title.

Library of Congress Control Number: Pending

May you live and die in love.

There are beautiful wild forces within us.

Let them turn the mills inside

and fill

sacks

that feed even

heaven.

- Saint Francis of Assisi

Half of all profits from the sales of this book will be donated to *Integral Without Borders*, a 501(c)(3) nonprofit, in service of those in need after the 2015 earthquakes in Nepal.

Contents

Part II: Midnight - 6 am

Part III: 6 am - Noon

Foreword

Feed Your Vow is a book I will always keep close at hand.

I will guard it fiercely, and give it freely. I bet you'll do the same. Because -the book you're holding springs geyser-like with so much of what we hunger for. These verses stretch their arms off the page, wrap fingers around your jaw, and look you square in the face. They found you right now, where you are, because they need to hear you laughing, feel you breathing, see you dancing.

It's a matter of life and death, really.
And love.

Like most visionary art, *Feed Your Vow* enacts its own imperative. Seeded in the title, it blooms on every page. If you meet these poems where they live, you will find yourself astonished, standing in the garden, surrounded by providence all along. Let's face it, some of us are starving. And it's easy to forget that hunger dissolves when we nourish others - a baby at the breast, a face in the mirror.

I'm no stranger to that bizarre state: needing to feed my vow, and not knowing how. I've been blinded to abundance by the quest for a morsel. I've scratched at dirt, oblivious to a canopy above, bursting with fullness. Amnesia has a lineage, too. Thank goodness for friends who free me from its rituals, reminding me:

Stop hoarding the blood-red wisdom unborn in you.

These poems study our perennial puzzles, but this artist slips us new clues: Hey, that missing piece - isn't that the shape of your own hand?

I knew Brooke McNamara for years without knowing she writes poetry. When she sent me this collection, I found out she writes *great* poetry. I spent the next few weeks reading, crying, laughing, sighing. Parts of me came home each time I sat down to read. I hadn't had that feeling - so clear, so strong - from a book in a very long time. I missed it. I need it!

I always knew Brooke to be a brilliant dancer, a dedicated spiritual practitioner. Amazing mother, wife.   She has a killer sense of humor; she's a kosmic source of love. All of that shines forth in *Feed Your Vow*, but also something else. A Presence. A winking, inside the within. It's a hallmark of mystical art. Ineffable, unmistakable. And it's here, refracted anew through the prism of this poet.

There are some books I return to again and again - *The Essential Rumi, Zen Mind, Beginner's Mind, American Book of the Dead.* They ring, just so, like a tuning fork I hold over my soul when I feel the pitch wandering.

Feed Your Vow - this poet's first book - is another I will return to, and re-tune to. It rings just so. Its pitch is true because it was forged in a source that can't be depleted, is never corrupted.

We have relationships with such books, like we do with people. Only a few particular loved ones are invited to experience everything with us. We want them at birthdays; we need them at funerals. We trust them with secrets; we shock them with surprises.

Feed Your Vow is that rare friend who will meet you wherever you are, as whatever you are, and resonate. You, hiding in shadows, under unbearable weight. You, invincible filament, shining love into the distance.

These poems don't quit half-way, claiming asylum in witnessing awareness. Their equanimity isn't passive. They put food into bellies, move blood into limbs. They remind us, like true tuning forks do: our body is a resonator. We are living instruments! Play, and be played.

You hold in your hands a clarion call to the tradition of love, animated in family, friends, fellow seekers - the locus of *We*. "We" is the only sure footing for a bunch of apes with angelic aspirations. *Feed Your Vow* brings us back, again and again, to the nearness of it: our solution, our salvation, is *each other*. Plural, infinite. Our prize is so simple, yet its ways are so subtle. We are always searching and arriving, together.

When I find a book like this, it feels like it's been here forever. Because what it conjures has, in fact, been here forever. That's the brilliance of this artist. Only a few lines in, walls are coming down, ears are perking up. Of course I want to hear this. I will always listen to this voice, because it issues from Home: my mother, my sister, my soul, my friend. How could it be any other way?

Books like this are one-in-a-million. That's why we guard them fiercely. But they're also a-million-to-one - in potency, in beauty. That's why we give them freely.

As a songwriter, I've spent my entire life following the way of words. *Feed Your Vow* leads me to an event horizon. Something powerful and unfamiliar, waiting for me on the other side. I don't feel I'm ready. I don't know if I'm willing. I only know it's a matter of life and death. I dream of delays, until a friend reminds me:

It's too late to be ready.
Erase yourself and remember the unknown as the love that's taking you.
Remember the love, my love.
Remember the love.

Stuart Davis
Artist
Boulder, Colorado

Introduction

Every poem is its own world. Disguised in these one-dimensional outfits of words on a page, we are tempted to think the poem wants to be treated ordinarily - to be read with ordinary attention. Not so. The poem wants intimacy with you; the poem wants extraordinary play. Every poem is a living being and thus wants living relationship. The fantastic part about this relationship is that it transcends some of the limits of human relating that can become tiresome and routine. The poem calls out:

Befriend me! Read me in the morning when it's quiet with a hot cup of coffee or tea. Let me give you a massage. Let me punch you in the gut to really wake you up. Read me outside, at the edge of the woods. Read me again right before bed with a soft gaze so I can enter your dreams. Let me confuse you so a new level of clarity can arrive on the other side. Read me again, slower, and slower still. Feel me in your body.

That last line is important. The poems that follow came from my body - which is not separate from mind - and they want to land as feeling tones in your body. Reading poetry as a practice to up-level our sensitivity toward and enchantment with this gorgeous, terrible world and our gorgeous, terrible selves requires embodied perception. It requires that we feel the language of poetry touching our private inner landscapes so we can become awake to the wisdom locked up or liberated in our flesh and bones.

The real beauty of reading poetry as a presence practice, the secret that keeps me coming back to drink this water-from-the-source, is that it *requires* my embodied perception, but at the same time *trains* it. The more I give, the more I get, so to speak. The more I wrestle and die with my favorite poets and poems, the more I perceive the rest of my world with full body-mind, sensuous curiosity and love. And then, at moments, this "me" perceiving "my world" dissolves into simple, undivided flow.

These poems were written for you.
I believe in an intelligence that brings together
writer, reader, and poetic landscape for reasons beyond our knowing.

So, if you are reading this introduction, these poems were written for you. Some of them are over a decade old and some are fresh from the past year, my first as a mother. Giving birth was a quest so miraculous and traumatic, so penetrating with unadulterated life force, that afterward I fell into a river of creative process I couldn't hold back. My experience of birthing was that of losing all sense of self in the process of going to an underworld to get my son, Lundin. On the other side, he was born gorgeous and I had a new body and mind that had been forced open to more light. My central vow in this life, I remembered, is to die to this moment so I can offer something to the world through creative process. This vow is one with the Zen Buddhist vows I've taken of awakening to service of all beings, and the marriage vows I've taken of devotion to one man as the focal point to break open and grow my heart.

What follows are artifacts from the practice of feeding my vow and my vow feeding me. They are also invitations to you to remember, create, feed and be fed by your central vow in this life, whatever it may be. Read these poems in order or at random; read one or all. They can only come to life through you - by means of your generous entrance into them, your time, your attention, and your willingness to feel. They need your mind to chew them so they can be digested by your heart. And in that process you and I commune across time and space - we know and are known, we love and are loved. This is the magic that truly feeds my vow. Thank you from the center of my heart.

Part I:

6 pm - Midnight

Stop with Me

Stop. Stop working. Stop trying to stop working.
Stop trying. Stop being lazy. Stop searching for meaning.
Stop landing anywhere. Stop acting confused. Stop.

Stop locking up your mysteries. Let me in. Stop rearranging the surface
features of your life. Stop thinking deep is deep. Stop thinking
blood is red. Stop hoarding the blood-red wisdom unborn in you.

There's got to be a better way. Do you love me? Stop
loving me. Stop unloving me. Stop tearing me apart.
Stop with me. Let's stop together. Six seconds. Ready. Set. Stop.

Now let's stop together forever,
and let the stopping go.

Medicine

Our massive, plastic brains
watch the ice melting
through our hot hands,
the gyres turning
their awful luminosity.

I want to receive anyone willing
in any condition
and love them full-bodied
till we fall to pieces and rain down
as God's broken heart
nourishing the good earth.

Change the Lighting

If you can't change yourself, after all
the efforts, change the light
by which you read your story.
Exchange overhead for something softer -
a lamp, a candle, a vine of shining
holiday lights - and feel yourself
become hugged by the fabric of shadows.
You see the darkness here has wisdom too.
You see these objects around become related
by the pregnant emptiness that holds them,
and you. Let this light reveal the rapture
of being just this. Then, further still, try
moonlight, or no light, until, at last,
this open, sourceless incandescence
which you are
no matter who you think you are
will follow you from the inside
wherever you may go, however
you may change, or not.

Avalokiteśvara

This poem is listening.
In that sense it is open.
Each word

is the surface veil
of a tunnel of listening
with no end or origin.

.

It receives
the things we think we hide:
the shine of awkward posture

when performing power,
the fervid care - too vulnerable
to share - hiding under small talk.

It hears the sighs
of your fifty trillion cells
living lucidly under your selfing,

and it absorbs your gossip also.
Give it the headlines of the day,
and the ache to fix it all. Give it

the story of your little you
and all the elaborate plans.
The kingdom and the ash.

Give the secret crisis
that pierces the center of all
us creatures here on earth,

these tenderized hearts
wise to the verity
of incipience and loss.

Say your full formal name
and expect no echo.
Say *yes*

to yourself
and listen
to the listening listening.

Mamacoke Island, Late September

We watch as the late light lengthens

every thing's shadow - every thing

moves with the heavy eyelid of the day,

gesturing surrender. This swan swims

like a memory, and the smoke from the boats

that slips into richness defines

the offerings of air. This is enough -

we know better than to fly

words into the fragile scene.

My hand is a blossom in your palm

as we watch each picture melt

into the next,

into the distance.

We see the coming darkness

as the sun's light heightening -

not a setting globe of flame

but a sky-hole, a hint

of that far world of divine fire -

this world that calls us

home

to burn in bliss.

One Act

My nose likes to point out
yours, flanking its right side,

and our lips, a little startled,
comment on their closeness.

Isadora

Nice, 1927

Before entering the convertible,

before passing up Mary's cloak

and Bugatti's coat, tossing instead the red

silken river of scarf around her neck

to alight along the back tire, before

"Adieu mes amis, je vais à la gloire!"

and the engine howl -

she spent a fine evening with friends.

On the couch, bones humming quietly inside,

she watched the old lover arguing finance

with two friends, their talk about the day

like always, but this time laughter

nudging from underneath, growing

like an unruly dance she could make, laughter

climbing conversation and flung gestures, laughter

lighting the lamp of old love, shining

up her spine to catch his attention through eye contact,

laughter breaking them,

making her bright blood ripple and perk,

pushing her up out of herself, with her friends

and her new old lover, that lucid evening,

before going out.

Story

Our holy planet keeps us close

     so as not to feed our bodies to infinity.

          We call her love gravity.

Why else make the effort

     to go up

          but to feel emphatic love falling?

Try to avoid her - look down - you fall

     again, each step we fall

          in love with her, every night

our tired bodies lie to meet her, asking

     what part we are.

          One day her love pulls us under.

Our Nature

I praise animal and I praise god, but I lay down my life
for that which gives birth to both. Why do we choose
to see and move from where we do? Some Indian lions
in this tv documentary, who even onscreen seem godly to me,
calm and delight my baby restless from twilight. He points
and yips at them sipping water or lazing in high heat.
I've pulled him in to me as darkness seeps in and deepens.
I'm moved by the patterns of fight and fornicate I see onscreen
that I feel linger in subtexts of human socializing. We watch
Macaque monkeys play and proliferate in the temple devoted
to the monkey god Hanuman, but fight when it's too hot
for pilgrims to come feed them. They flash teeth and brawl
over water, space, and mate. I think of the women
who've come on to my husband while I was pregnant
or home with the new baby - how part of me loves them,
but most of me wants to kick them hard where they are soft
and scratch their blush-colored cheeks till they bleed.

It's dark now; my baby's come in closer for milk.
The monkeys rest after fighting. One mother sits nursing
her little one in perfect mirror image to our position.
She gazes out, tired and tousled, and I watch myself
watching us all. A spiraling current sneaks up my spine.

CircumScribe

I once was a graffiti artist up all night hunting
and circling scenes of random beauty.
I'd tag my name underneath:
CircumScribe.

It was a dream.
It came from infinity.
It landed in my marrow.
It made my bones light.

It reminded me: the last time I died
I was born Brooke Julia Gessay
October 9th, 1981, and the gap
between is the gap happening now.

It reminded me: I was born with a vow so central
it can't be seen, beating my heart, and my job
is to live it to certain death. It reminded me:
we must feed our vows with our very own flesh.

It reminded me: circle beauty. Move bones
by moving the gap inside the marrow.
It reminded me: it's not all going to be ok,

but it already is, but I must make it so.

It reminded me of the hours I failed at birthing
in the bardo between night and day, and how
I gave up trying, so bewildered by terror and intensity
until that thin veil appeared between this world

and what's under it - that darkness unfathomably full -
and the silent voice sounded
everywhere and nowhere
are you willing to die for this?

and I yowled the *YES* that changes everything
while pushing a planet down and out my pelvis
and a big bang, different but similar, ripped
through my throat with a violent ultraviolet light.

It reminded me: there are resources
we cannot conceive of, and we find them
in the asking if the asking
is alive enough to annihilate

and reorganize our current selfing
for something better at love.
It reminded me: I see you
bravely meeting what is yours

alone to meet. *Are you willing to die*
for this? Feed your vow
and eat it
and offer it away.

- CircumScribe

Part II:

Midnight - 6 am

Please Send Signals

If you're reading this,
which you are,
I wonder if you're sitting

on the cold fifth floor floor
of the library, as I did in college,
either full of or hungry for euphoria,

surrounded by books of poems.
Where is a recipe of words
that will bring me to a delicious boil?

The small, hot phrase I can carry
like a molten berry
strung up in my heart

to light these heavy days?
Or perhaps you're standing
at the ocean's edge near midnight,

reciting Dante to a numinous moon,
and drinking the distance
to the dark horizon

till heartache gets a little undone.
Maybe we all feel homeless
here on earth

till someone or something teaches us
to plunge headlong straight into
the raw longing for home.

If you're still reading this,
which you are,
please send signals

back to young me
to keep going into the night -
fill the space around her and the books

with your playful presence,
send a shooting star that she'll just barely catch
from the corner of her left eye.

The Best Dream

You right now
waking up

to play the part
of love's guts.

Blush

I must begin with what I really want.
I want to let the mess be. I want you
to show me your world. I want to push
the weight of my real body into your world
and feel the impact. I want to show you
my naked electric power and watch you fall
to your knees in worship. Enter my kingdom
so I may be peopled with life. Show me the one
in you that makes me shimmer between fear
and awe. Give me the white heat of loss
to carve me down. Trip me over traps I've set
to remind me this is just a dream. Pain, come
reveal again this dream is also real. Dreams, be each night
of Chögyam Trungpa Rinpoche, and wake me to a new mind.

I want to train your perception
to encounter how achingly erotic
that tree being swayed by the breeze is.
I want to train your breath
to move that holy arousal into your true purpose
and aim it like an arrow at my lies.
I want you to shut up and come close
and let me taste your tears.

Angel of Impermanence

for Severen Bailey Schoew

She writes the words.
Miscarriage. My baby died.
Hear that timeless carnal wail!

What force takes human form
and leaves it in one
grand and seamless gesture?

The crossings
of the threshold
mark us all forever.

Angel of Impermanence!
Thank you
for teaching us what cannot be known

except by depths of heart -
for branding us
with this burn of the beyond -

and for the pain
that sends us back to our source

to ask:

Who is the knower of pain?
Who is here for all that comes,
as well as all that goes?

Nobility

When someone close is laboring
and we cannot make it go away -

when someone close is suffering
and it's not ours to remove -

perhaps we can simply witness with awe
as if a quest had been given by the Queen,

and its fulfillment is sacred transmutation.
Please remember: this is not the only world.

Fever

The virus purrs
my baby's breathing
and I hold him, my heart
dying

to soothe, cracks
to a trillion glittering soldiers
who storm his world,

stand up
in his cells and say
love like this
does not look away.

They'll wait
beyond time,
immovable and unarmed,

for the hot seed
of wisdom
at the core
of this fever.

Hildegard of Bingen and Jeffrey Dahmer

Sometimes I wake
to what seems an announcement -
one simple, clear thought in words -

Six weeks ago: *Hildegard of Bingen,*
my mind declared. Today: *Jeffrey Dahmer.*

Whatever the message, I take it
as a clue to know myself more.

Uplift to study Saint Hildegard, twelfth century,
also known as *Sibyl of the Rhine*, born sickly
and offered to the church, visionary,
composer, musician, writer, creator of morality plays.
"The shade of the living light," her first vision, arrived
at age three - at five she said she sensed all things
in the light of God; when she died at eighty-one
some sisters saw two streams of light above.

Now, nausea, studying Dahmer, twentieth century,
also known as the *Milwaukee Cannibal*, born with borderline
and raised in tension, found guilty of murder,
rape, dismemberment, cannibalism, necrophilia.

As a boy he captured carcasses and took them apart
to see how they "fitted together"; condemned as a man
to sixteen life sentences, he terrified even the other inmates,
one of whom killed him at age thirty-four.

The two figures stand side by side in my mind,
which has to relax open to hold them both
at the same time.

In a ceremony too holy
to understand,
they turn to each other -

NO MORE!
WAKE UP!

she bellows
with ferocious,
cataclysmic love -

and they touch hands lightly,
and begin to merge.

Brazen

Sometimes my care is paralyzing
or saccharine, impotent
in its need to look a certain way.

This is when I have to say
fuck it
a few times, because *fuck it*

is the plug to
fuck me
into something past an image

of sweetness into something able to rise
volcanic, move my fury
into splattering, igneous wisdom

and pour over all our bullshit, nullify
to reveal innate radiance.
Fuck it - my love can kill.

Every Light Becomes Lighter

When darkness draws sudden and absolute
into every vein, pulses new species of panic,
stains inside organ lining, locks into lactic acid
knotting muscle that clutched

on for survival, when darkness rages reason
into shattered gravel, when darkness rages,
how can we source resilience but as Dante
to that first morning star after hell:

O sun which clears all mists from troubled sight,
such joy attends your rising that I feel
as grateful to the dark as to the light.[1]
I thank blood

that courses toward eyes alive to see
the past as past (it *has* passed, *has*),
and live grateful, grateful - oh God,
thank you! - grateful for it,
all.

Why Dance

Every wall can be entered. Imagine

we can trust our pleasure. Imagine that
free fall of fullness won't break us,
or that the breaking will bring us
only more kind and brazen, refined
and reordered for a higher order of this
being human. I don't know. Silence
is the deepest form of pleasure.

Why dance? Would you ask me why
I'm painting the night purple?
We animals want color, or the sensation
of color. Sometimes our wilderness
wants to be witnessed, and silence dancing
is the deepest form of color.

Are you still here? Do you remember the attic
of your childhood home and how you hugged
the ghosts that rose in the dusty light
of your dancing? Imagine you could trust
that fullness falling breaking you open
and knew that dancing

is the deepest form of silence.

Imagine that

ticking sound ceasing and our waking to see

nothing

but this dancing, and the dancing

never ends so *quiet now*, it's time to enter

that impossible wall,

and pass through so dazzled

we forget the lie that we're separate.

Part III:

6 am - Noon

Interruption

I love to wake early and sip strong coffee
and sit like a queen in the dark
and ask my death to reach back and teach me
so I can write down what I hear. If I listen
with my whole spine, the currents
of deep grief and wild arousal wash me
to a more original body. So I sneak
out of bed early this Christmas eve,
and float to the kitchen to percolate
in my husband's parent's home, past
the blind dog sleeping in her crate,
great-grandma's bedroom
where little girl dreams dissolve
even as they form translucently around her
in the dark dry morning air.

I come back to our room
triumphant with my mug,
set up my cushion, and hear
Lundin, 8 months old, pile of sleep squirming -
snortling and milk-hungry, my husband's hand on his heart
to soothe. Back-bending and flapping arms that thwack
pillow and little protruding belly, stretch that furrows

the brow and pooches the lips and makes a tiny

tremble through the absurdly adorable body,

and I'm called

to my first purpose, to feed

from my own body, to feel

these rivers of simple service that destroy

ideas of who I think I am pull

from my bones and pour

into his little suckling lips.

My desires are silent as I give up

writing this morning, and lay here instead,

my hand petting his hair, everything

for the moment effortless, awestruck

by death's teaching today.

Discipline and Roaming Free

Once mind is remembered
to be infinite
the difference between discipline
and roaming free
is nothing.

We become empty
enough to be filled
with rich freedom-responsibility
of being and serving
all of it
and just this one
at once.

I feel my feet
on this hard wood floor
and breathe you in.
We make and discover
each other, always only
in this moment.

Tell me: do you have a body
right now?

Dust Hums

Beneath the birthday breakfast left
on our living room table, in longing
light that shadow-spills dusk
in windows, upon the orphaned
note: *love-you-fiercely*
and along the lip of lotus,
dust hums.

Dust,
under the child's uneducated foot,
in the velvet fold of moth wing,
the temple bell. Through the hand
of realization that rings it, the honeyed
highlights of your right eye,
across soft plains that wait
to burst into rice kernel,
around the refining curve
of your candlelit plans,
dust purrs its prayer.

Dust-song, engine that croons along,
hides in snow on tracks that slide
a train home, fills the space you lived in

and left, sifts in soil raked up by storm.

It plays Duke Ellington
in a purse of American letters
on a bench in the woods
behind the Castello Pasquini.
Covers us
and comes from us,
from the staggering man's mantra: *love
is a verb*. Reverberates. And hums here
where your life inter-animates mine.

For Nothing

I wait for nothing in these early hours

as the earth turns to receive the heat of sun.

There is no time to write this so I turn

into the folds of dark to seek my nothing

where even the clocks have dozed off. I drop

the pen and behold my open hand. I arrange myself

just so. I lean back over bottomless canyons

inside myself until all that's left

is ancient hunger

for the falling

into nothing

and the sweet, refulgent rebound

of his rising to fill me until

I'm gasping within this un-mixable mixture

of nothing himself pressing into my inner body,

swimming like an orca up through my little hips,

the spark in my heart dangerously ablaze,

my head bowed listening down to sip the mystery.

I wait for nothing because he alone is large enough

to hold me, from the inside's inside,

and touch me where I am secret

wide open nothing too.

Bell

for Dorothy S. Hunt

"I had been my whole life a bell, and never knew it
until at that moment I was lifted and struck." - Annie Dillard

I woke up, opened a notebook, and wrote:
What do I want? - paused, unhinged myself,
and let three words fall through: *A true teacher.*

After work I wandered beyond my Fillmore bus stop,
following my fancy, onto an unknown street, into an unknown
bookstore, and right to an unknown emerald green

book of poems. The words, straight from silence, struck
me as the bell I didn't know I'd always been -
and I'm ringing still:

because there's no beginning, this throbbing never ends.

Dive

My genius is still sleeping in the wall to our left,
dreaming again of William Butler Yeats

and his island of Innisfree, which crossfades to your face
describing desires: relief and release: that colorful

cafe on the hill that eternally lures you
with the lofted living space where you could go

and stay awhile, and get some rest, and walk out
into the various shades of green all morning,

come home to read or write with tea or coffee, the ocean
right there bringing song and the perfumes of change -

but also that untold tidal wave always rising, relentless,
the constant question of when it's time to dive.

Heartgasm
for Rob

When we met

my heart popped

and I died

of gladness

and then everything

was born

now.

Little Blue Boat

Timelessness is a little blue boat
that follows me wherever I go.

One glance toward it, one step in,
and the I that drives me softens off.

The boat also dissolves
from its role as a noun

to its being as verb
and we are instantly in love,

always outside the hours.
Objects nearby join us in waking

into this living dream:
jade plant waking wooden chair

waking thin blue nightie
on the hook on the wall all

waking. Together we turn
to behold my husband and son

sleeping in these early hours
and they too have dropped

their apparent permanence
instead to shine, pellucid.

Their chests rise and fall:
big one, little one, rising, falling.

Nothing else but this watching,
receiving. Nothing else but this.

Oh, unbearable sweetness.
Oh, sweetest grief!

Enactment

How does it feel
to let yourself

be lived
by God?

Morning Eyes

Lundin blinks open
his eyes
and they are spacious as an angel's,
portals straight

to the heart of it. Slowly
a warm layer of his personality rolls in
to fill the pupils, then the splash of humor,
then all

the unique patterns
of his particular toddler-ness -
and then he's here.
And then he's off.

Writing After Not Writing

I invite myself shyly

as if to a crush

to pause

and sit

and see if there is something real

to say. It is a confrontation

so startling and intimate

a bit of me recoils - a sea anemone

brushed by an other's touch.

Then, dawn.

Soft surge

of crackling happiness.

It does not matter so much

what we say

but how -

if the words come rising

on a wave

of core longing, core being -

if this great and faceless

attention shines forth.

Reality is not a metaphor.

The doors are all

flung open.

Writing in Red on Paper Towel

Ordinarily I type, a smooth pecking
of my fingertips filled
with nerve endings and longing
for truth: quick, arhythmic

flutterings and lappings, happy
prancing - sometimes stomping -
and every so often a pause
while suspended in a gap

between thoughts, as they do
on you, when I am telling tales
through your skin,
that full-but-almost-not touching

on low back, face-frame, or hands,
where stillness and anticipation
mean more than any movement,
pure heart-mind pouring

through each tingling finger
like a wizard conquering evil -
but now I'm stranded

without laptop

so stray paper towel and red pen
are my utensils -
into the pressed, textured fluff
I inscribe myself to you:

freehand red rhapsody, freewheeling
vermillion wishes, blessings of sanguine
contact however you want it -
subtle or strong.

I write to you tenderly
on stained paper with flawed magic wand,
which bleeds these words
instead of spells.

Letter from my Last Letter to Mel

I'd always wanted to be written by Rilke
or Van Gogh, but I did enjoy the way
you spelled me well and made me a little
musical. I'd heard of the ones that went
between Miller and Nin, and imagine
my making - so hot and continuous,
so neat to sloppy - akin to theirs.

I love my generous length and how
you riddled me with gems of truth
you didn't know you'd give.
Perhaps you held back a bit
with how hard it's been
with your partner: I feel myself
always choking there.

But the place near my middle
where you went to New York
and met mountains inside yourself
you'd never yet climbed -
you began to let my hair down
there and then (curious
lightness!) the words

don't matter

by my end - you've got me

jigging and singing

and tossing up wine

and Mel must feel the same for you

because I'm softer now

and my folds crack from the daily reading.

The Other Side

Waking on my back,
the first impression of this day is weight
on my low belly -

the back of my toddler's head
settled there,
instead of nestled in my armpit,

his body sprawled out off to my left,
basking on his back
in some radiance

seemingly available only to sleeping babies.
The humor strikes me
even before fully awake,

as if we've connected in some perpendicular paradise,
two abandoned *tetris* pieces
landed accidentally on this bed,

or been hired to pose for an Annie Leibovitz spread:
Vanity Fair doing a piece
on one-year-old's remembrance of the womb,

how they'll nuzzle up

in reverence and nostalgia,

in full backward prostration to mama's belly,

dreaming of the good old days

of buoyancy and warm water,

of distant, muffled voices

from those two

whose love means everything,

the constancy of chord

for companionship and food.

Life was so simple back then -

his sleeping posture seems to express -

before exploding into this new world

made more of effort

than fluidity, of distances

that must be crossed,

full of warnings and hungers,

contrast and collision.

But there *is* something about this place -

his sudden stirring
begins to say -

those faces lit with adoration,
the instant, constant party
of moving in this body,

chewable, smear-able food,
kisses, creeks, dancing,
dogs, and grass! - yes,

it is worthy here too -
his squirming toward consciousness
starts to declare -

this is good, this is good,
this is good again
to wake here this morning,

to have arrived so long ago,
through the harrowing journey out of mother
to this, the other side.

Part IV:

Noon - 6 pm

Encounter

You there.
Have you forgotten something?
Something about choosing?
Look around: is this the world
you promised yourself?

I want to know who you could become
if the conditions were just right.
I want to know the you that's possible
with just enough thunder
and just enough sun.

Who taught you the human smile,
and did it ever land
in the living tissues of your human heart
beating miracles for free -
or is your face always onstage?

When you speak do you hear that one
as the oldest friend
since your microcosmic firework of conception,
which made creatures of the earth and sky alike
shudder with jollity and not know why,

or does your own voice

still sound to you like a stranger?

I want to know if you need permission

to arrive home right now

into your body longing to learn you.

Do you know breath

as always a holy door?

Who are you when you breathe

down deep, at last allowed to feel it all,

and your hair bursts into flame, and you remember:

we don't choose once and it's over,

but are asked to re-engage in every instant.

Look around: this very world

needs your arrival now, like sun

and like thunder, now and now and now.

33 Ways to Get Better at Not Getting Better
and So Possibly Really Get Better

The force of love is eating you alive, whether you align with it or not.

Also, you're going to live forever.

Forever here is defined as up until the end of you.

Always erase the second to last sentence you just heard.

Become earnestly curious about the character and life-span

of dust bunnies.

Always erase the second to last sentence you just heard.

Let your shadow lead you out walking near mountains and rivers,

and fade in and out of shade.

Finishing and beginning, beginning and finishing, making and erasing,

erasing and making.

Every new gesture contains a core of no-trace.

Let this no-trace lead the cooking of eggs and asking of hands.

Invite Dogen Zenji for breakfast and ask his hand in marriage.

What is reality? An icicle forming in fire.[2]

Tomorrow will be.

Tomorrow will be yesterday.

Tomorrow will be yesterday erased two sentences later, leaving no-trace.

Sit till you feel forever moving.

Move till you feel forever settle into yesterday.

Praise the way your mind is melting into more.

Note the ways in which you make yourself like a cave.

Praise the cave with a trap door into a perspective that's empty of eyes.

Follow cake-crumbs in the dark one gulp at a time till you fall through
a trap door into a birthday party just for you.

It's all for you.

It's all for you, my love.

But don't forget: you're going to live forever.

And let me just say this plainly: you don't know.

Hear it like a heavy hole in your heart that will lead you home.

You don't know!

Hear it like the only real inheritance you've got, the only one that well
befriends the finishing of you.

Let going go.

It's too late to be ready.

Erase yourself and remember the unknown as the love that's taking you.

Remember the love, my love.

Remember the love.

To My Future Daughter

2002

Any day might become your birthday
so I celebrate each.

Many steps before your entrance
through me and into skin,

I think of your face - all wind
and wanting - and how

it guides me to the high hill
on which you wait.

A white moth flutters
where your heart will grow,

one bamboo shoot
describes your spine.

Meditation on Motherhood

Crying breasts.
Crying baby.
Crying sky.

Milk,
tears,
rain

all moisten
and bring forth
what's coming

into being.
All we have to do
is the very next thing.

Strawberries

In seeded jackets
they practice patience:
plump into red royalty,
translating sunlight.

A slow combustion
gives the green arm
a whole heart to hold on to,
which asks nothing

but to be sweet wealth.
Where is the definition
of benevolence
except inscribed in these bodies,

in the ruby juice
they'll always bleed.

Sleeping on Apricots

The poetry
of the moment
is how we're sleeping
on apricots.

Your hand from behind
contains my navel,
your nose
in my occipital pool.

We'll nectar
to death you say;
it's the pits
we giggle,

and dream on
top the squashed
jammy fuzz
of new love.

Un

Today, after a lunch

of leftover noodle soup, I flew

a parabolic path

up mist-made mountains

into a slate-grey sepulcher of weather.

Through the fog I rode the backs

of twenty seven pelicans, leaping

from each to each.

Lights from our little island

were flints of glitter

beneath the clouds,

our city a distant myth.

I whispered your name into the esophagus

of the first black hole I found

and never made it home

to tell the tale.

My love for you is a tame little thing.

Looking

Digging through Lundin's diaper bag again

    I find one thousand diapers, not enough

        wipes, twelve sun hats and twelve winter hats,

nine sets of extra clothes, twenty-one mismatched socks,

    sippy cup spilling in slow motion, toys talking

        to teething tablets, enough crumbs

for two adult dinners,

    two hundred towels, a tractor, extra jacket,

        extra shoes, extra stroller, extra crumbs,

extra leaking, extra teething, extra extra,

    a chicken

        that comes to roost on my shoulder,

a memory from fifth grade, a longing, a poem

    begging to be written, and then

        Saint Francis of Assisi himself, luminous around the head,

whom I pull up by the armpits

    to stand beside me, gazing down.

        The bluebirds on his shoulders

chirp to my chicken; the fawn curled up

in the crook of his arm wakes easily.

Long pause. Deep, loving eyes.

"The one you are looking for

is the one who is looking," he says,

and turns to boil some water for tea.

Circling Back

What is your perennial strength?

Remembering source.

That relates to your tenacity.

What do you mean?

You know how to get what you want.

How?

By remembering source.

Coffee Date

The old friend tumbles in,
hair a state of mind. The light
apology. The *it's okay*.
The order and the coins.
Our drinks become spiked
with stories: words pour into air
like coffee from the pots; we watch
the game of thought-tag heighten, knowing
we have signed on to too loud laughs,
a quickening ride of words.

Outside
rain runs
to make love to loam:
liquid needles pierce soil
and thread back up as grass.
Coffee was only an excuse.
What we want? Each others' eyes
smiling as our tales wriggle together
on the playground of the table, to remember
where we went before we came
apart, to dip past the depth of laughter
into sudden drunken love -

old and private, one garden growing

in two separate hearts.

We only want to watch the rain

together again,

the silence falling

as if always.

Command

My boundaries tell me

      when they've been crossed; I know

            my sense of self is offended

when a flare goes up

      from the little army

            fear has been training

in my nervous system since the beginning,

      and a four-dimensional

            wave of rage rolls out

from some source in my solar plexus

      to all the edges of my territory.

            Now, the difficult question:

is the intelligence of the moment

      to declare war

            in protection of my self and my truth,

or surrender it all

      to Life's sacred attack?

            I do have a choice.

Buoy

Let go.

Stay awake!

For Anneka

The word *coach* comes from *kocsi*
after the village in Hungary in the 1500s
where the thing originated which carries beings
from one location in space to another.
The newer layer of meaning
was born later from slang

at Oxford University, *coach* becoming
what I called you if you tutored me,
and thereby *carried me* through an exam.
Next emerged the version
relating to athletics - the quality
of passionate calculation for the win,

the possibility of which gives birth to loss,
never appealed to me in naming my work
as an audaciously-labeled *life coach*.
But the old meaning helps me now,
as I sit silent with news of you having been born
into the realm of memory. Four days ago you died,

the kind of young and lovely and feral
that feels impossible to believe.

My second ever life coaching client,

I sought to subtly carry you toward clarification

and fruition of those central longings,

and presence with everything

that seemed an obstacle

in the adventure

of you becoming you.

I remember the gift of getting to listen.

I remember being heard. Now I feel

only your boundless presence smiling

and our roles reversed,

as I silently invite you to coach me

from the other side. Maybe you'll teach me

that death is not out there

but in here - maybe you'll carry me deeper

toward wherever you are now

that I may be blessed by it

and thereby bless - blossoms

from the other worlds

falling out my pockets

for we who suffer to love well here,

and need carriage along the way.

Window

This is not a poem

for right now; I'd like to read it

when I'm dead. It might not last -

it might get bored waiting

and move to New York to make art

out of patterns that connect.

It might wander into a hall there to hear

sublimely rendered Arvo Pärt, a sound reminiscent

of the childhood canyon with the tree with the perch

for a wider view on things. The poem tells me

it wants to roam: Ulaanbaatar and Rome are calling!

I'll follow it anywhere, even to my exit. We are allies.

I want it to tell me when I'm on that other shore, unmade,

that I may climb back through it

like a window

into this life again.

In the Middle

Of beginnings,
middles,
and endings,

it is middles I find hardest to enjoy.
Beginnings so drenched in the miracle of novelty,
endings so vivid with nostalgia and loss,

middles can't help but seem linear
and lame by contrast. In the middle,
human attention will so easily walk away,

like the popular girl in middle school
in search of something cooler.
That's why right here

as we enter these middle stanzas
it might be skillful to add something dazzling -
perhaps drop a peacock here in line fifteen,

male of course, sauntering through, whose azure,
cobalt, and golden feather tips subtly alight
in the twilight breeze to distract you

from the boredom threatening

here at the middle; maybe his torso's luster

and tail fan's fanciness could even keep you

inspired in the middles of long March work days,

in the lull of half-done projects losing steam

or romance losing steaminess. I want a close up

on our peacock here, as we come toward the end,

to abruptly peck and pierce through

these lines, to show us they can be full of empty

spaces that breathe between the words. I want

to surprise you when you find out this bird

is a Zen master in disguise - as all things are -

whose squawking you suddenly recognize to mean:

Waking dwells in all directions -

boredom holds the gift -

there is no such thing as beginnings -

there is no such thing as

The End.

Acknowledgements

I first thank my beautiful and wise mother, Marci Pilatti, for birthing me into this world and holding me every moment after in love and respect. Mom, I've grown in the light you've beamed on me and the space you've held. There's no greater gift. Thank you for my life and for laughing with me along the way.

This book quite literally would not exist without the generosity of my husband, Rob McNamara. He gave his knowledge and experience with publishing freely so that what I've written could move out into the world. Rob, thank you for touching your forehead to the ground at my feet and offering me your life. I love and worship your great heart.

My first readers gave time and attention to these poems that they probably didn't have, being the busy, amazing people that they are. April Glaser, Lauren Mitchell Wilkinson, Deb McNamara, Nataraja Kallio, Jenna Gessay, Erika Randall, Jeff Salzman, Ariel Polonsky, Maria Bailey, Danielle Lanslots, Lily Dwyer Begg, Kelly Notaras, and Aline Wachsmuth: thank you for the reflections you offered that carved, blossomed or spiced these poems. Lauren Beale, thank you for guiding me in metabolizing feedback wisely. I loved working with each of your particular ways of perceiving, and I was buoyed by your care in the process of refining.

I thank my father, Glenn Gessay, for his immense love and intelligence. Dad, thank you for engaging my mind with riddles and card games as a child, and for your interest in my writing now; thank you for your deep care and wit. I wish you happiness and send you love always.

I thank my siblings, Ryan Gessay and Lauren Slater Major, for making me strong and funny, as well as sensitive and attuned, by having grown up around their brilliance. You two are guides for me, each in your own way, and much of who I am (which streams into this book) I owe to you.

Gratitude to Portia Snow for sharing her haunting photograph for the cover of this book. I love your raven sky wrapped around these poems. Heartfelt thanks to Alex Musat for both strength and flexibility in designing the cover. Thank you for going back and forth and back and forth with me. I love you and bow deeply to your aesthetic brilliance.

I offer thanks to my writing and poetry teachers: Charles O. Hartman, Gideon Rappaport, and Mark DiTargiani. Each of you has called me forth and given the gift of mentorship. This has, at moments, literally saved my soul. Thank you also to my college cohort who helped me refine some of these older poems: Melissa Mylchreest, Geoffrey Babbitt, Lauren Mitchell Wilkinson, Andrew Seguin, and Ian Abrams.

I also thank the writers that get me out of bed before dawn to meet them through their work, and then teach me what's important: Billy Collins, Galway Kinnell, Jane Hirshfield, Mark Strand, David Whyte, William Bronk, Annie Dillard, Anne Lamott, Mary Oliver, Rabia, Hafiz, and Rumi. Each of your voices - some combination of human and beyond - has reminded me of who I am and why I am here. There are no words for my gratitude for how you have influenced me.

I offer infinite thanks to Stuart Davis for his crazy, wakeful art that keeps me laughing hysterically and perfectly disoriented. You, my friend, are a genius. Thank you for all of your mind blowing support and for writing a foreword that inspires me to actually publish this book. Thank you for envisioning me writing more books after this one.

Friends and family whose names I have not written, thank you for your support in countless, selfless ways. You know who you are; I love you. I also offer thanks to my personal family ancestors for going before me and creating a path to enter this precious human life. I bow to the lineage of zen ancestors to which I belong - the women and men who have for centuries carved a groove of wholehearted practice that lines me up with deepest intuition. And enormous gratitude to Dragon Heart Sangha for being my practice family in this lifetime and walking into the beautiful fire together again and again.

My first teacher, Dorothy S. Hunt, whose vivid and unwavering presence appeared in my life quite magically and brought the deep currents from background to foreground, is forever etched in my heart. Thank you Dorothy; everything opens into the ocean of love through the portals of your eyes. I wish there were proper words for my gratitude.

I want to thank my guides in the subtle realm who keep me sane, connected, and inspired. Thank you also to my own body for sharing its voice so clearly.

I cry as I offer gratitude to my teacher, Diane Musho Hamilton, whose embodiment of beauty and truth have redirected the course of my life since the moment I encountered her. Sensei, thank you for receiving me, reflecting me, dismantling me, and empowering me to inhabit my humanity fully with an open heart. I love you in and as this one mind.

And Lundin, my sweet boy, thank you for coming to be my son and become the human being you are meant to in this world. Thank you for carving through my very body a path of service. So much of this work is inspired by you - thank you, my adorable little muse. I have wanted to be your mama since forever.

Notes

1. Italicized quotation from: Dante Alighieri, *The Inferno,* trans. Robert Pinsky (New York: Farrar, Straus, and Giroux, 1994), Canto XI, lines 91-93.

2. The lines *"What is reality? An icicle forming in fire"* and *"It's too late to be ready"* from: Zen Master Dogen, *Shobogenzo: Zen Essays by Dogen,* trans. Thomas Cleary (Honolulu: University of Hawaii Press, 1986).

Resources

Brooke McNamara offers classes, workshops and performances in the fields of creative writing, dance, yoga, and meditation, as well as one-on-one coaching with emphasis on creative and contemplative practice. To learn more or to contact Brooke, please visit:

www.FeedYourVow.com